Using Lib

Workshops for Family Historians

Stuart A. Raymond

Published by the Federation of Family History Societies (Publications) Ltd.,
Units 15-16, Chesham Industrial Centre,
Oram Street, Bury, Lancashire, BL9 6EN, U.K.

Copies also obtainable from:
S.A. & M.J.Raymond,
P.O.Box 35, Exeter, EX1 3YZ, U.K.

First published 2001

ISBN: 1-86006-144-3 (FFHS (Publications) Ltd)

ISBN: 1-899668-19-5 (S.A. & M.J.Raymond)

ISSN: 1033-2065

Printed and bound by Alpha Print
Crawley Mill, Witney, Oxfordshire OX8 5TJ

Contents

Acknowledgements 4

1. Introduction 5

2. Your Personal Library 7

3. Using Libraries 9

4. The Internet 16

5. Archives 17

6. Publishers 18

7. Journals and Newspapers 21

8. Source Publications 23

9. Conclusion 32

Front cover: The New Reading Room, British Museum

Acknowledgements

My thanks go, firstly to all those who have stimulated my interest in genealogy, books and libraries over the years. Sue Lumas kindly read an early draft of this pamphlet and gave me some ideas; Bob Boyd has seen it through the press. My thanks too to the officers of the Fedeation of Family History Societies, without whose coooperation this book could not have been published.

Stuart A. Raymond

1. Introduction

The library is the genealogist's workshop; books are the tools of his trade — along with journals, microfilm, and CDs. Archives are also important, as is the collective memory of the genealogist's own family. And, in its place, the Internet is a useful tool. But most of the information needed to get started will be found in books and other published materials: they will point you in the right direction, and are essential tools for the genealogist. You need to know how to find them, and what they may tell you. You need to consult them before you visit the archives, and discover the advice they can offer. One of the first things you need to do when beginning your research is to read an introductory guidebook to genealogy; as you proceed you will find that there are innumerable indexes and transcripts of original sources available in published format, there are many guides to specific record offices, and to particular categories of source material such as census returns or parish registers. There are brief biographies in published biographical dictionaries for millions — yes, millions — of individuals. Many thousand genealogists have completed their research (if it can ever be called completed!) by publishing their family histories or pedigrees in book form or as journal articles. The information contained in published materials is absolutely vital for genealogical research. Yet so often the importance of books and other published materials is ignored by genealogists, and, indeed, by genealogical authors who ought to know better. So often, beginners head straight for the archives, rather than consulting printed materials first. The consequence? Needless wear and tear on irreplaceable manuscripts, waste of time for the genealogist, and failure to identify every link possible.

This pamphlet is intended to provide you with guidance on the use of books and libraries. It tries to answer a number of questions — or at least to point you in the right direction.

- What genealogical information can be found in books (and other published formats)?
- How can genealogical books be identified?
- Where can they be found?
- How should genealogists use libraries?

This book is not, however, a substitute for Raymonds *English genealogy: a bibliography,* or for the other books in the British genealogical library guides series (see the back cover for details of these). It is not the intention here to offer a definitive listing of all genealogical books that are available; that is totally impossible in the compass of 32 pages. Rather, the aim is to suggest a route through the maze of genealogical books, libraries and publishing.

2. Your Personal Library

If you intend to be serious in pursuit of family history research, then you need to start building up your own personal genealogical bookshelf. This does not mean that you should purchase every book that you need to consult. It does mean that you should aim to have close at hand those books which you are likely to consult repeatedly. At a minimum, this would include a good general introduction to genealogy, a dictionary or encyclopaedia of the subject, and a bibliography. Each of these deserve some discussion.

Introductory Texts

There are many good introductory texts to choose from; a fairly full listing is given in Raymond's *English genealogy: a bibliography,* although several new books have appeared since that was compiled. When choosing the text to suit your needs, the criteria you should consider are comprehensiveness, accuracy, date and price. Sometimes the more expensive texts do not justify their extra cost by extra content. Accuracy may not be easy to judge for the beginner, but you do need to be aware that not everything you see in print is correct. Be aware, too, that the genealogical world is constantly changing: you need a text that takes into account the most recent developments, such as the establishment of the Family Records Centre by the Public Record Office. It is also useful to check whether the text contains a decent bibliography – some, amazingly, fail this test.

I cannot offer a comprehensive listing of introductory texts here; the most authoritative guide is now:

- HERBER, MARK D. *Ancestral trails: the complete guide to British Genealogy and Family History.* Sutton Publishing/Society of Genealogists, 1997.

Dictionaries/Encyclopaedias

The genealogist is likely to come across terms which he does not understand, or topics on which he/she needs more general information. What is an inquisition post mortem? Who was Hardwick? When were censuses taken, and why? These sorts of questions can be checked out in a good genealogical dictionary. Surprisingly, only two such dictionaries are on the market, and one or other of these should be considered essential for the genealogical bookshelf. They are:

- SAUL, PAULINE. *The family historians enquire within.* 5th ed. F.F.H.S., 1995. New edition forthcoming.

- FITZHUGH, TERRICK. V.H. *The dictionary of genealogy.* 5th ed., revised by Susan Lumas. A. & C. Black, 1998.

Saul's volume tends to offer a more popular approach; Fitzhugh is more academic — and probably more useful.

Bibliographies

This word has already been mentioned once or twice. Don't be frightened by it! A bibliography is quite simply a list of books. And without an adequate listing, how are you going to identify those books which are relevant to your research, given that there must be at least 100,000 books and journal articles likely to be of interest to the genealogist. Good bibliographies are an essential part of any genealogists library.

Almost the only up to date and reasonably comprehensive listings of genealogical publications are in the *British genealogical library guides* series. Raymonds *English Genealogy: a bibliography* is a select list of published items of potential relevance to all English genealogists; the county volumes in the series aim to provide comprehensive coverage of all local publications. These are works which you should be consulting repeatedly, so you would be well advised to purchase the national volume, and the county volumes for the areas your ancestors come from. They include details of books, journal articles, fiche, and CDs on a very wide range of subjects: history, bibliography, archives and libraries, journals and newspapers, names, biographical dictionaries, occupational sources, pedigrees, family histories, parish and nonconformist registers, probate records, monumental inscriptions, lists of names, directories, religious records, estate and family papers, governmental archives, education, emigration, and much more. If you need information on any of these subjects, the first thing you need to do is to find out whether it has been published. And if you need to undertake a systematic search, then you need a systematic listing of the sources that need checking. That is the reason why you need to consult bibliographies.

3. Using Libraries

It has already been suggested that there are over 100,000 books and journal articles likely to be of use to British genealogists. Of course, you could not possibly own them all! But you do not need to. Libraries provide public store-houses of books. They exist in order that you can consult the books you need.

How should the genealogist approach a library? There is a tendency to expect both too much and too little. Too much, in that family historians often expect librarians with little experience of genealogy to be able to follow the interminable twists and branches of their own family tree. Too little, in that they do not know what level of service it is reasonable to expect, and tend to accept poor standards as being the best that can be offered.

When you visit a library, how do you behave? Do you try to sneak in unnoticed? Do you hesitate on the doorstep? Or do you march up to the issue desk and ask the junior clerk on duty to show you how to use the Index Library's indexes to wills? All three approaches are wrong. They are based on mistaken assumptions about the role of the librarian and his junior staff. It is the role of the professional librarian staffing the information desk to answer questions. You should therefore never be afraid of wasting the librarian's time by asking your question. Indeed, if you do not ask it, you are preventing the librarians from doing their job. However, it is as well to be prepared with the right question for the right person. Many people are employed in libraries who are not professional librarians. The first member of the library staff you meet is likely to be a junior clerk who knows not much more about libraries than you do. You can ask the junior where the non-fiction collection is housed, or how many books you can borrow, but it is extremely unlikely that any junior clerk would ever have heard of the Index Library. So be sure that you ask a professional librarian those questions which require professional knowledge.

How can you use the expertise of a professional librarian? What response can you expect? In libraries catering primarily for genealogists, they will be experts. But as a general rule, librarians faced with a genealogical inquiry will cringe, then smile, and then do their best to be of assistance. What you have to remember is that they are not genealogists. Most know very little about genealogical sources, and cannot be expected to provide you with detailed instructions on how to conduct your research. You are the researcher; it is up to you to master genealogical research techniques. Librarians cannot do that for you. What they can do is to help you track down information available in published sources, whether it is in their own library or elsewhere. Librarians do have a great deal of expertise in the retrieval of information. They should be able to tell you whether the Cornish protestation oath rolls of 1641/2 have been published, and, if so, where you can consult them. They should be able to give you the bibliographic details of a book on the Tucker family of Devon published in the 1980's. They should be able to help you search indexes to journals, biographical dictionaries, and newspapers. And they will, of course, be able to outline the resources of their own library, and to explain how their catalogue is supposed to work. They should be able to do all of these things whether their library is in London or Cape Town, Melbourne or San Francisco.

The library catalogue is the key to the book collection of any library, and you should make it your business to understand it. Catalogues normally enable you to search by author, by title, and by subject. The catalogue entry will provide a full bibliographic citation to the item sought, giving you at least author, title, place of publication, publisher, and date of publication, together with the call number. Most libraries use the Dewey system of classification, and it is worth remembering that the Dewey class no. for genealogy is 929 — although you need to be aware that useful material could be classed elsewhere. English history, for example, is 942; books on the bibliography of English genealogy will normally be found at 016.929, the prefix for bibliography being 016.

In most libraries, the catalogue is now computerised. Do not be misled by this into thinking that the information the computer holds is complete. It may not be. It is impossible to computerise a library catalogue overnight, and some libraries which use computers still rely on card catalogues to access books acquired before computerization. In other words, you may need to consult at least two catalogues to ensure that you have seen all relevant material; in some cases it might be three, or even four. And there may be specialist catalogues too; for example, Devon has a county-wide computerised catalogue, but the West Country Studies Library, which is part of the system, has a separate catalogue of its own holdings. Ask the librarian for guidance on what catalogues are available.

Library catalogues provide access to books. They also provide access to periodicals, but they do not normally provide access to articles appearing in periodicals — although this is not always so. Methods of identifying articles in journals are discussed below.

The value of a library catalogue to you as a genealogist is, of course, dependent on the size and subject coverage of the collection. If the book you require cannot be had in your local library, you may be able to buy it, or find it in some other library, or get another genealogist who does have a copy to check it for you: there are a number of sites on the internet dedicated to lookups, and you can also ask for help on newsgroups or mailing lists. If all else fails, you can ask your librarian to obtain a copy by tapping into the inter-library loan system — but be aware that there may be a cost involved, both for you and the library. If you have access to the internet, you can yourself check the holdings of a large number of academic and other libraries on-line. The books in the Surrey History Centre, for example, are all listed in the Surrey County Council catalogue, which is available in this way. Remember that the catalogues of most county library systems include the holdings of libraries throughout the system; for example, the catalogue of Hampshire County Library lists collections of all the libraries in the system, including those in Winchester and Portsmouth.

Libraries are run by a variety of different institutions: local and national government, universities, societies, even the Church of Jesus Christ of Latter Day Saints. Each library has its own particular strengths, which it pays to be aware of.

Public Libraries
Public Libraries usually have many branches, including a local studies collection; the latter is likely to be of major importance for genealogists who are tracing ancestors from within the library's area. The aim of the local studies librarian will be to collect everything that has been published relating to the area; in addition to the books, there will be the transactions of local and county historical societies, publications from family history societies (perhaps including microfiche) and edited texts from the county record society. In general, the function of the library will not include maintaining a collection of archives; that role is normally performed by County Record Offices, although in some instances, e.g. the Surrey History Centre and the Suffolk Record Office, the roles of local studies library and county record office have been merged. The local studies library may, however, hold some unpublished material; for example, the West Country Studies library holds many transcripts of wills and inquisitions post mortem, and its Burnet Morris index is of major value in tracking down historical information on Devon.

Local studies libraries are not necessarily the only public libraries in a particular county or borough to hold useful genealogical material. They are concerned with the particular locality — but genealogists may have roots hundreds of miles away. The West Country Studies Library is one of the first

11

places for genealogists with Devon roots to visit — but if your roots are in Shropshire or Yorkshire, the Exeter Reference Library next door is more likely to be of use to you, with its substantial collection of record society publications, historical and archaeological society transactions, and published parish registers from throughout the nation. Reference libraries will generally hold major sources such as the *Times index* or the *Dictionary of National Biography*.

University Libraries
The family historian should not neglect university libraries. You should check admission requirements, but most allow public use — although a fee is payable in some cases, and in a few cases references may be required. In the case of the Bodleian Library at Oxford, new readers also have to swear an oath not to deface any book! Those universities which have interests in British history are likely to have extensive runs of the journals of county historical, archaeological and record societies. They are also likely to hold some of the major county and local histories for most counties. In addition, you should not neglect the historical bibliographies to be found on their shelves. Many of them cover a much wider range than genealogy, but genealogists need to be aware of the wider historical disciplines. The university libraries of Oxford and Cambridge have the right to receive a copy of every book published in the UK, and consequently their collections are particularly extensive.

The British Library
The British Library also has the right to a copy of every book published in the UK. It is the largest library in the UK, and the second largest in the world. Its British genealogical collections are probably more extensive than those of any other library. There are very few items listed in Raymond's bibliographies which are not available in the British Library — apart from the microfiche publications of family history societies, which have not been systematically collected. In order to gain admission, however, you must demonstrate that you cannot easily obtain the books you require anywhere else. The library's catalogue is available on the internet at **www.blpc.bl.uk**. It is also worth consulting the older printed version of the library's catalogue (with the warning, of course, that it only includes material published prior to the date of its own publication):

- *The British Library general catalogue of printed books to 1975.* 360 vols + 6 supplementary vols. Clive Bingley, et al, 1979-87. Some libraries may have an earlier edition.

The arrangement of this massive compilation is different from the on-line version, and also from most other library catalogues. It is primarily alphabetical by author, but has many peculiarites useful for genealogists. Family histories, for example, are sometimes identified by family name rather than by author; the library's extensive collection of trade directories are all listed under the heading Directories; publications related to particular societies and organizations based in particular places e.g.churches (including works such as parish registers) are listed under the names of those places; the extensive collection of regimental histories and related works are listed under England: Army; reference to the heading 'England: College of Arms' will lead to a detailed listing of the pedigrees of the gentry drawn up at heralds visitations. There is much, much else, and every genealogist would be rewarded by spending an afternoon with this work, which is available in most major reference libraries. The point is not so much to identify books in the library itself (although that may be useful), as to identify titles which may be found in a number of other libraries, or in booksellers catalogues. Who knows, you may come across authors in your family tree whose books are listed there.

Family History Society Libraries

Family history society libraries are rather different. These generally began in the bedrooms or garages of members, but many societies now have their own premises and are able to open their libraries on a regular basis. A few years ago, the major strength of these libraries were their collections of 'exchange' journals from other family history societies. Unfortunately, space constraints have resulted in many of these collections being drastically reduced. The F.F.H.S. have undertaken a programme of microfilming family history society journals, and F.H.S. libraries ought to be encouraged to ensure that fiche of exchange journals are kept. The major value of F.H.S. libraries today are the resources that have been created by their own members — transcripts of monumental inscriptions and parish registers, indexes of census returns, collections of pedigrees, and so on. They also usually have small collections of local history publications, but these generally are not comparable to the collections found in public libraries. A handful of societies publish catalogues of their collections. A listing of the resources of family history societies nation-wide is currently in preparation.

Society of Genealogists

The Society of Genealogists runs the F.H.S. library par excellence. Its collection includes innumerable published transcripts of original sources; it also holds thousands of unpublished transcripts of parish registers, monumental inscriptions, and other sources. The society's microfilm collection is probably the best collection of its kind in the U.K; in addition to the microfiche publications of most family history societies, it also holds numerous microfilm copies of original sources, and many indexes, such as the I.G.I. the General Register Office indexes of births, marriages and deaths in England, 1837-1920, the Bernau index of names appearing in court records, and other items too numerous to mention. Catalogues of a number of its collections have been published; for example, census indexes, parish registers, monumental inscriptions, directories and poll books, school and university registers. — although these would be more generally useful if it were made clear which items have been published and may therefore also be found in other libraries. The Society of Genealogists is one of the few F.H.S. libraries with a computerized catalogue, which will eventually be available on the internet. The advent of the 21st century is also acknowledged by its collection of CD-Roms. It is worth noting that a number of its unpublished indexes are available on the internet at:

- English Origins
  www.englishorigins.com

The society's own web page is at
- Society of Genealogists:
  www.sog.org.uk

County Historical Societies
County historical and archaeological societies frequently have good collections of local histories. Many of these societies exchange journals with each other; consequently, they may have extensive collections of the journals of county historical societies nation-wide. Hence their libraries may have much more than local value, although frequently their existence is overlooked by family historians. The libraries of societies such as the Somerset Archaeological and Natural History Society or the Yorkshire Archaeological Society are invaluable to the genealogist.

Family History Centres
The Family History Centres of the Church of Jesus Christ of Latter Day Saints are able to tap into the resources of the world's largest genealogical library in Salt Lake City, Utah. Each centre holds a catalogue of the Utah library, and is able to order microfilm from there. A vast amount of original source material is available — parish registers, civil registration indexes, wills, monumental inscriptions, and a wide variety of other sources. There is a small fee for ordering, but this is far out-weighed by the cost of consulting these records in

any other way. The library catalogue can be purchased on CD, and is also available at:
- FamilySearch
  www.familysearch.org

British branch libraries are listed on the internet at:
- Family History Centres
  www.lds.org.uk/genealogy/fhc/

Locating Libraries

It is the argument of this book that any librarian should be able to direct you to information likely to be of use in genealogical research. Nevertheless, it is important to remember that many libraries do specialise in the subjects they cover. The strengths of some libraries have already been pointed out, but there are many others; for example, Sutton Libraries have a particularly strong genealogical collection. Despite the title, a full list of local studies libraries is included in:

- COLE, JEAN, & CHURCH, ROSEMARY. *In and around record repositories in Great Britain and Ireland.* 4th ed. Armstrong Boon Marriott Publishing, 1998.

A variety of similar listings of libraries and resources are available: ask your librarian for these. Alternatively, a number of gateways to library webpages are available on the internet; these are discussed in the next section.

Library rules, o.k!

Do as you would be done by is the golden rule in libraries, as elsewhere. Bear in mind that most of us prefer silence when concentrating on our research. Bear in mind too that other people may want to consult the books you use (and you may want to consult them again as well). So handle them with care, avoid marking them in any way, and remember that food and drink, whilst they may mean life to you, mean death for books when brought into libraries. Always check opening hours, which do change surprisingly frequently; check too whether you need to book equipment such as fiche readers in advance. Finally, if your researches end up in print, do donate a copy of your work to the library where you did the research for it.

4. The Internet

To a degree, the internet now competes with books and libraries as a source of genealogical information. However, the content of the majority of internet sites — with honourable exceptions such as Genuki (www.genuki.org.uk) and the Public Record Office site (www.pro.gov.uk) — would easily fit into small pamphlets, rather than substantial books. Basic and valuable information is available on thousands of sites, but very few sites include substantial original source material such as is available, for example, in the many publications of record societies (see below). For a useful introduction to the Internet, you should read:

- CHRISTIAN,PETER. *Finding genealogy on the internet.* David Hawgood, 1999.

Using search engines to find particular sites on the internet can be tedious; the majority of searches tend to throw up hundreds, if not thousands, of results. In the same way that we all need telephone directories, we also need published internet directories. That is the principle underlying:

- RAYMOND, STUART. *Family history on the web: an internet directory of England & Wales.* F.F.H.S., 2000. To be regularly updated.

One feature of the internet which is particularly relevant in the present context is the fact that hundreds, if not thousands, of library catalogues can be accessed through your web browser. A chapter of *Family history on the web* is devoted to listing library and record office web-sites; here, mention might be made of two of the most useful sites for identifying books and libraries:

- *Familia*
  www.earl.org.uk/familia
  Familia offers an extensive listing of genealogical resources in libraries, and is particularly valuable for its notes on the holdings of particular libraries.

- BUBL UK
  www.bubl.ac.uk
  Links to the catalogues of innumerable national, public, and university libraries are provided here.

5. Archives

Archives are primary sources for genealogists. Much of the information in genealogical books is derived from them. But that does not mean that you should consult them first — far from it! There are a number of basic distinctions between books and archives, which need to be understood. Firstly, archives are unique. There can only be one original register of births marriages and deaths for any parish; any other copies are just that — copies, which are not necessarily accurate. Consequently, archivists need to take much greater care of their archives than librarians do of most of their books. Archives cannot be put on open shelves! And, in the interests of preservation, genealogists should only consult them when it is essential to do so. Secondly, archives were created for administrative purposes, and not for genealogists. The fact that they would, in course of time, provide vital evidence for the family historian was of no concern to the administrators who designed census returns. The researcher needs to understand the administrative background to the origin of particular sources, in order to understand what they say, and, just as importantly, what they do not say. Thirdly, archives are often unindexed and unlisted, and may be very time-consuming to identify and search. Many collections have, of course, been listed and indexed, but many more lie untouched.

Archives are generally not to be found in libraries, although this is not a hard and fast rule; mention has already been made of a number of instances where record offices and local studies libraries have been combined. Most record offices have small libraries of their own, but these are frequently intended as much for staff as for the public. Before county record offices were created, some libraries collected archival materials, and some of these collections may still be held. Also, many libraries do hold manuscript materials, for example, unpublished histories, or manuscript transcripts of parish registers and monumental inscriptions. Whilst not, strictly speaking, archival in character, these do share some characteristics with archives, including their uniqueness, and their frequent lack of indexes. For further information on archives, reference may be made to:

- LUMAS, SUE. *Basic facts about ... archives.* F.F.H.S., 1997.

6. Publishers

New genealogical books are coming off the press thick and fast! For publishers this is a growing market, and they are keen to take advantage of it. Nevertheless, the major genealogical publishers are non-commercial organizations. The F.F.H.S. and the Society of Genealogists both play a major role in encouraging authors to get into print, and in trying to ensure that the genealogist has the books needed to pursue the hobby effectively. Both have extensive lists of their own publications, and both, incidentally, also sell many publications from other sources. Their web sites are invaluable sources of information on current genealogical books:

- Federation of Family History Societies
  www.familyhistorybooks.co.uk
- Society of Genealogists Bookshop:
  www.sog.org.uk/acatalog/welcome.html

A major role in genealogical publishing is also played by numerous family history societies, many of whom are engaged in producing transcripts and/or indexes of original sources such as parish registers, monumental inscriptions, and probate records. Much of this output is on microfiche rather than in printed form, and a microfiche reader is a useful adjunct to any genealogist's library. Those researching in Kent and Lancashire are particularly fortunate in that there are well over 1,500 fiche for each county published by the local family history societies.

Most current family history society publications are listed in two works produced by the F.F.H.S. (be sure you use the most up to date edition — otherwise you may miss out on recent publications):

- HAMPSON, ELIZABETH. *Current publications by member societies.* 10th ed. F.F.H.S., 1999.
- PERKINS, JOHN. *Current publications on microfiche by Member Societies.* 4th ed. F.F.H.S., 1998. New edition in preparation.

The web-sites of societies are also worth checking for more up to date information; these are listed in Raymond's *Family History on the Web* (see above). Alternatively, they can be identified at two internet sites:

- Genuki
  www.genuki.org.uk/Societies/

- F.F.H.S. List of Member Societies
  www.ffhs.org/members

Record Societies

A major role in genealogical publishing is played by record societies. Some of these are national bodies; others cover particular counties or regions. Their function is to publish calendars, indexes and transcripts of archival sources, many of which are of major importance to genealogists. The most important for our purposes are probably the British Record Society's Index Library, which publishes indexes of probate records, and the Harleian Society, which concentrates on pedigrees from heraldic visitations, and formerly also published parish registers, especially of London and Middlesex. The county and regional societies are also important; many wills, for instance, have been published by the Surtees Society, and the Devon and Cornwall Record Society issued numerous parish registers in its early days. Innumerable deeds, tax lists, ecclesiastical records, and a wide variety of other sources, most of them of relevance for genealogists, have been edited for record society publications; a full listing is published in:

- MULLINS, E.L.C. *Texts and calendars: an analytical guide to serial publications.*
  Royal Historical Society guides and handbooks 7. 1958. Supplement 1983.

An update to this covering publications issued since 1982 is available on the internet at:

- Texts & Calendars since 1982: a survey
  www.hmc.gov.uk/socs.list.htm

Libraries and Record Offices

Libraries and record offices also produce important publications for genealogists. Guides to record offices, lists of parish registers and other sources held, editions of particular sources, and indexes to archives all provide invaluable information. Some of the Public Record Office's publications are important for all genealogists, e.g. *Tracing your ancestors in the Public Record Office; Never been here before? A genealogists guide to the Family Records Centre.* Essex Record Office has an extensive publishing programme, which includes many volumes of sixteenth and seventeenth century probate records. The Borthwick Institute's *Texts and calendars* series (no relationship to Mullins's work), and other publications are invaluable sources for the northern genealogist. You should inquire what publications have been issued by institutions in the areas from which your ancestors came — they might just prove useful.

Commercial Publishers

Commercial publishers have an important role to play in genealogical publishing. The name of Phillimore immediately leaps to mind. W.P.W. Phillimore published an extensive range of marriage indexes in the early years of the 20th century; the firm which bears his name continues to publish a wide range of family histories and research aids, although it is now chiefly interested in local history rather than genealogy. It is worth obtaining a copy of its current catalogue.

Other major publishers, e.g. Suttons (publishers of *Ancestral trails*) occasionally issue genealogical books, but the most interesting material published commercially tends to emanate from smaller publishers. For example, Bill Galloway Publications have issued numerous parish registers and other source materials for Somerset; Original Indexes produce, as their name suggests, innumerable indexes of original sources for Northumberland and Durham, mainly on microfiche (so do Northfiche); innumerable British trade directories have been reprinted on microfiche (in Australia!) by Nick Vine Hall; S.A. & M.J.Raymond have reprinted quite a number of pollbooks of the eighteenth and nineteenth centuries; Janice Simons is reprinting extracts from the extensive births deaths and marriages columns of Norfolk newspapers – the list is endless! It is worth finding out who is publishing what in the area(s) from which you think your ancestors came.

CD publications

The last few years have seen an explosion in the publication of genealogical information on CD. Probably 1,500 genealogical CDs are currently available from about 70 different publishers, mostly commercial organisations. Most of these CDs make available published sources which have long been out of print – especially trade directories and parish registers. Very few contain material which has been compiled specifically for CD publicaton – although those that have are mostly of major importance, e.g. the F.F.H.S's *National burial index.* An attempt to list all published CDs is made in:

- RAYMOND, STUART A. *British Family History on CD.* F.F.H.S., 2001.

7. Journals & Newspapers

There are numerous journals of value to family historians. *Family tree magazine,* which is a commercial production, the *Genealogists' magazine* from the Society of Genealogists, and the F.F.H.S.'s *Family history news and digest* are the best known general titles, and are all worth reading regularly. The Public Record Office's *Ancestors* is a new venture in this field. Virtually all family history societies publish a journal or newsletter for their members; these usually include notes and news on current events, members interests, and articles likely to be of general interest, or reporting research on particular families. The 'digest' section of *Family history news and digest* provides regular indexing of the articles in these journals.

It is still worth checking back runs of the major genealogical journals published in the nineteenth and early twentieth centuries. These contain numerous family histories, pedigrees, and transcripts of sources. The major titles were the *Miscellanea genealogica et heraldica,* the *Genealogist, The Ancestor,* and the *Collectanea genealogica et heraldica* (which became the *Topographer and genealogist*). The contents of these journals are listed in:

- RAYMOND, STUART. *British genealogical periodicals: a bibliography of their contents.* 3 vols. in 5. F.F.H.S., 1991-3.

A number of other general historical and archaeological journals of the same era carried articles of a similar nature. The genealogical content of the *Associated Architectural Societies reports and papers,* the *Archaeologia,* the *Archaeological journal,* the *Journal of the British Archaeological Association,* the *Northern genealogist,* and the *Reliquary* , are listed in:

- RAYMOND, STUART A. *British genealogy in miscellaneous journals.* S.A. & M.J. Raymond, 1994.

The genealogist and the local historian share many interests in common, and the transactions of county and local historical and archaeological societies frequently contain articles of value to the family historian. Dont be put of by the word 'archaeological': its usage has changed since the nineteenth century, when it was closely allied with genealogy. Numerous family histories, transcripts of sources, and other information of genealogical value are to be found in these transactions. Many of them have been published continuously since the nineteenth century, and most have published detailed indexes of their contents covering many issues. Good collections of these transactions are frequently to be found in university libraries and in the libraries of the societies themselves (as noted above); some public libraries, e.g. Exeter, the Guildhall Library in London, also hold many of these titles.

Genealogists and the general historian also have interests in common, and general historical journals occasionally carry articles of genealogical relevance. These can be identified in:

- *The Royal Historical Society bibliography on CD-ROM.* Oxford University Press, 1998.

This incorporate two older works:

- *Writings on British History.* Royal Historical Society, et el, 1937-86.
- *Annual bibliography of British and Irish history. Harvester Press for the Royal Historical Society, 1976-* .

It may also be worth checking:

- MULLINS, E.L.C. *A guide to the historical and archaeological publications of societies in England and Wales, 1901-1933.* Athlone Press, 1968.
- *British humanities index.* Library Association, 1963- . This continues the former *Subject index to periodicals,* and recent years are available in electronic form.

The most comprehensive listings of genealogical articles in all types of journals are provided in the county volumes of Raymonds *British genealogical library guides.*

Newspapers are much more difficult to use, although they can be valuable sources of information for the family historian. Very few have indexes, so it is necessary to have some idea of the dates which are likely to have relevance before you begin your search. Most local studies libraries have runs of newspapers for their local area; the British Library's repository at Colindale has the major national collection. For guidance on the use of newspapers, you should consult:

- CHAPMAN, COLIN. *An introduction to using newspapers and periodicals.* F.F.H.S., 1996.
- COLLINS, AUDREY. *Basic facts about ... using Colindale and other newspaper repositories.* F.F.H.S., 2001.
- The British Library Newspaper Library
  www.bl.uk/collections/newspaper/

This site includes many links to other newspaper sites, as well as the library's catalogue.

8. Source Publications

Transcripts and indexes of innumerable genealogical sources, such as parish registers, wills, tax lists, and the census., are available in print. The pattern of publication varies with the particular type of source, and the following notes may prove helpful.

Parish Registers

These are a major source for genealogists, partially indexed in the I.G.I Many record offices have published lists of their own holdings, and the county volumes of the *National index of parish registers* provide comprehensive lists of original registers, bishops transcripts, and modern transcripts. Many family and local history societies are active in transcribing and indexing parish registers, but unfortunately only a small proportion of their work is actually published: most are lodged with the originating society, with copies (perhaps) to the relevant local studies library and the Society of Genealogists. There are, however, a number of major published series. The *Phillimore parish register series* included transcripts of hundreds of marriage registers from throughout the country. Over 100 registers were printed by the Parish Register Society. Many London registers have been published by the Harleian Society. In Lancashire, Yorkshire and Staffordshire there are societies exclusively devoted to the publication of parish registers. Such societies once existed for a number of other counties: Surrey, Durham and Northumberland amongst them. Some registers have also been published by record societies such as that for Devon and Cornwall. In Bedfordshire, all registers prior to 1812 have been published by the County Council. Currently, a number of family history societies are publishing registers on microfiche, e.g. Kent Family History Society, and some of the Welsh societies. Many private individuals have also made major contributions to the publication of parish registers; in most of Raymonds county bibliographies, a glance through the section on parish registers will reveal the names of editors who have transcribed or indexed many registers for the county concerned – Bannerman in Surrey, Cotterell for Middlesex, Dwelly in Somerset, Crisp in Suffolk (and elsewhere), and many more.

In 1908, G.W.Marshall produced a national listing of published registers, but he has had no adequate successor. The Society of Genealogists has produced a listing of the register transcripts it holds, but unfortunately this does not make it clear which registers are published, and gives totally inadequate bibliographic citations, so that it is not of any use to those unable to visit the Society. The most comprehensive listings of published registers are to be found in the county volumes of Raymond's *British genealogical library guides.* Reference may also be made to his *British genealogical books in print* and *British genealogical microfiche,* to John Perkins' *Current publications on microfiche from member societies,* and to Elizabeth Hampson's *Current publications from member societies.* Between them, these four volumes list all published parish registers currently available. Many older published registers, e.g. most of the Phillimore series, have recently been re-published on CD; these are listed in Raymond's *British Family History on CD.*

For parish registers published by record societies, reference may be made to Mullins *Texts and calendars* (see above). Parish registers published by a variety of other societies in the early part of the 20th century are listed in Mullins' *Guide* (see above), and in the many volumes of *Writings on British history.*

Memorial Inscriptions

These are another valuable source of genealogical information, but they have not been published to the same extent as parish registers or probate records. Family history societies are currently producing many fiche editions of inscriptions; for these you should consult the latest edition of Perkins *Current publications on microfiche.* Numerous inscriptions were published in the columns of local historical society transactions in the nineteenth and early twentieth centuries; some of these may be identified in Mullins' *Guide* (see above) but there is no adequate listing for the 19th century, apart from Raymonds county bibliographies. For the same period, many inscriptions were published in national genealogical and historical journals such as the *Genealogist,* 1877-1922 and *Miscellanea genealogica et heraldica;* these are listed in Raymonds *British genealogical periodicals: a bibliography of their contents.* 3 vols. in 5. F.F.H.S., 1991-3, and its supplement, *British genealogy in miscellaneous journals.* A small number of general collections of inscriptions are listed in Raymonds *English genealogy: a bibliography.* Comprehensive listings of published inscriptions may be found in Raymond's county bibliographies.

Probate Records

Wills and their associated documents — inventories, administration bonds, and executors accounts — are of major importance for genealogists, and many publications have been based upon them. The basic guide is:

- GIBSON, J.S.W. *Probate jurisdictions: where to look for wills.* F.F.H.S., 4th ed., 1997.

Record societies have published numerous indexes and some texts of probate records. The British Record Society's Index Library includes over 100 indexes to wills proved in particular courts. Societies such as the Staffordshire Record Society and the Lincolnshire Record Society have printed a number of collected editions. These may be identified in Mullins' *Texts and Calendars*. Universities — especially those where local history is taught in extra-mural departments — have also produced collected editions, as have a small number of commercial publishers and private individuals; these may be identified in the *British national bibliography*. Many individual wills have been printed in local history society transactions, and are listed in Mullins' *Guide,* in the *Subject Index to Periodicals,* and in the *British humanities index.* Those included in family history society journals are listed in the 'Digest' section of *Family history news and digest.* Many family history societies have published will indexes and transcripts on microfiche; for these, check Perkins' *Current publications on microfiche by member societies.* The most comprehensive listings of published probate records are to be found in Raymond's county bibliographies.

Lists of Names
Lists of names are invaluable sources for tracing the distribution of particular surnames, and for identifying the places in which it might be worth undertaking further searches for your ancestors. The census is the most important such list, but there are many others. Tax lists, the protestation and other loyalty oath rolls, pollbooks and electoral registers, etc., are all valuable genealogical sources.

The Census
Census schedules are now widely available on microfilm in public libraries. A full nation-wide index to the 1881 census is available in most major libraries, and we are promised internet access to the 1901 census shortly. A CD edition of the 1891 census is also in preparation. Family history societies have produced innumerable indexes to the censuses for other years, as pamphlets and on fiche; these are listed in Perkins *Current publications on fiche,* and Hampson's *Current publications by member societies.* Raymond's county bibliographies provide comprehensive listings, including indexes from other sources as well. The best collection of census indexes is at the Society of Genealogists; this is fully listed in:

- KENYON, G. *Census indexes in the library of the Society of Genealogists.* 3rd ed. Society of Genealogists, 1997. Unfortunately, this does not give any indication as to whether particular indexes are published, and, hence whether they are available in other libraries or for purchase. It is therefore only of use if you are using the Societys collection.

For the location of microfilm copies of the census schedules themselves, you should consult:
- GIBSON, JEREMY, & HAMPSON, ELIZABETH. *Census returns 1841-1891 in microform: a directory to local holdings in Great Britain, Channel Islands, Isle of Man.* 6th ed. F.F.H.S., 1994.

Tax Lists
Numerous tax lists, and especially rolls for the subsidy and the hearth tax, have been published by record societies; these are listed in Mullins *Texts & Calendars* (see above); many are printed in the major county historical & archaeological societies *transactions,* whose indexes are worth checking. Full listings are provided in Raymonds county bibliographies. It is worth noting that a major effort to publish surviving hearth tax returns is currently under way at the University of Surrey's Roehampton campus.

Loyalty Oaths
Loyalty oath rolls are another valuable source. The protestation of 1641/2, when Parliament and the Crown were competing for the loyalty of the English, required the signatures of the entire adult male population. Where returns survive, this amounts to a census of all adult males. The House of Lords Record Office holds most surviving returns, although coverage is patchy. Most surviving returns have been printed, and are listed inRaymonds county bibliographies. A complete listing of surviving returns, and of printed editions, may be found in:
- GIBSON, JEREMY, & DELL, ALAN. *The protestation returns 1641-42, and other contemporary listings.* F.F.H.S., 1995.

Poll Books
Pollbooks provide similar lists for the 18th and early 19th centuries. By an act of 1696, sheriffs were required to prepare lists of voters and how they cast their votes; many of these lists were published at the time, although some remained in manuscript. The franchise was limited, so these volumes only identify relatively substantial inhabitants (in the counties, only owners of land worth over 40 shillings per annum). Nevertheless, they usually list many thousand names. There are major collections of pollbooks at the Guildhall Library and the

Institute of Historical Research; some are also held by the Society of Genealogists and the British Library, and in the relevant local libraries and record offices. Few have been reprinted in recent years; *Raymonds Original Pollbooks* series is the only major reprint series in book form. A few have been reprinted on fiche by family history societies, and by Brookes Davies & Co. One or two are available on CD. Modern reprints may be identified in Raymonds county bibliographies, and in the various guides to fiche and CDs listed above. For a full listing of extant pollbooks, see:

- GIBSON, JEREMY. *Poll books c.1696-1872: a directory to holdings in Great Britain.* 3rd ed. 1994. This also lists modern reprints, but is now rather out of date in this respect as a number have appeared since 1994.

Electoral Registers

Registers of Parliamentary electors were required by the Reform Act of 1832, and have been published annually since then, apart from the years 1916-17 and 1940-44. They may be found in libraries throughout the country, but very few have been republished in recent years. The only substantial reprint known to the author is the *Somerset Electoral Register 1832,* published by S.A. & M.J.Raymond in two volumes. A handful are available on fiche, and may be identified in the fiche listings mentioned above; they are also listed in Raymonds county bibliographies. A national listing of original electoral registers and their locations is provided by:

- GIBSON, JEREMY, & ROGERS, COLIN. *Electoral registers since 1832, and burgess rolls.* 2nd ed. F.F.H.S., 1990. Unfortunately, this volume does not include the collection of the British Library, which is extensive.

Trade Directories

These were the nineteenth century equivalents of the modern telephone directory, providing listings of the more substantial inhabitants in each community mentioned. Trade directories tend to be scarce, and may only survive in the local studies library for the area covered. The British Library has a major collection of directories; the 'Directories' volume of the *British Library general catalogue of printed books* provides a full listing. The collection at the Society of Genealogists is listed in:

- NEWINGTON-IRVINE, NICK. *Directories and poll books in the library of the Society of Genealogists.* 5th ed. Society of Genealogists, 1995.

The Guildhall Library also has a good collection of trade directories, which were microfilmed by E. P. Microform in the 1970's; part or all of the microfilm collection may be available in other libraries. A number of other commercial publishers have also microfilmed early trade directories; these are listed in Raymonds *British Genealogical Microfiche*. Trade directories have been very popular with CD publishers in the last couple of years; their publications are listed in Raymonds *British Family History on CD*.

Trade directories are listed in Raymonds county bibliographies; however, for comprehensive national listings, with locations, consult:

- NORTON, J.E. *Guide to the national and provincial directories of England and Wales, excluding London, before 1856*. Royal Historical Society guides and handbooks 7. 1950.
- SHAW, G., & TIPPER, A. *British directories: a bibliography and guide to directories published in England and Wales (1850-1950) and Scotland (1773-1950)*. Leicester University Press, 1988.

For London directories, see:

- ATKINS, P.J. *The directories of London 1677-1977*. Mansell, 1990.

Estate Records

The records of estate management — deeds, leases, surveys, rentals, accounts, manorial records, etc — constitute a vast seam of unmined evidence for family historians. Much has been published, but far more remains hidden in the archives. Exploration of what has been published, however, may yield invaluable information for the genealogist. Many collections of deeds, court rolls, and other estate records have been calendared for publication by record offices and record societies (Mullins *Texts & Calendars* — see above — should be consulted for the latter). Many have also been published as articles in county historical and archaeological society journals (see chapter 7). The latter also include many manorial descents based on, and with extracts from, estate records. Manorial descents were a staple diet for many 19th century local historians, and most county histories published prior to the early 20th century include detailed notes from estate records seeking to prove such descents. Many such works can be identified in Raymond's county bibliographies.

Ecclesiastical Records

In previous centuries, the church was much more involved in society than it is today. Parochial government was in the hands of church-wardens, the clergy were involved in the rites surrounding virtually all births marriages and deaths; the ecclesiastical courts supervised the administration of probate and the morals of the populace. Everyone was touched by ecclesiastical activity in some way. I have already discussed probate records and parish registers, but a variety of other ecclesiastical records are also available in print. Churchwardens accounts, bishops registers, the records of various ecclesiastical courts, lists of clergy, and similar materials have been published in profusion by record societies and county historical and archaeological societies. All of these provide valuable information for family historians; detailed listings can be found in Raymonds county bibliographies, and in Mullins *Texts & calendars . . .*

Quarter Sessions Records

The major role in county government prior to the late 19th century was played by quarter sessions. Their records are preserved by, and form the core collections of, most county record offices. Some of the latter have published calendars and indexes of the records in their care, as have many record societies. These are listed in Raymond's county bibliographies, and in Mullins *Texts & calendars ... .* Useful listings may be found in the *British Library general catalogue of printed books* under the names of counties. Reference may also be made to:

- GIBSON, JEREMY. *Quarter sessions records for family historians: a select list.* 4th ed. F.F.H.S., 1995.

Occupational Sources

If you know what your ancestor did for a living, then it may be possible to locate information on him by consulting sources related to particular occupations. There are numerous biographical dictionaries, descriptions of particular archives, record publications, professional society membership lists, trade directories, genealogical guides, and similar publications. Works such as these of national interest are listed in:

- RAYMOND, STUART A. *Occupational sources for genealogists.* 2nd ed. F.F.H.S., 1996.

Separate volumes giving similar local information deal with *Londoners Occupations* (2nd ed., 2001), *Yorkshire occupations* (2000) and *Surrey & Sussex occupations* (forthcoming); similar local information may also be found in Raymonds other county bibliographies.

Family Histories & Pedigrees

The aim of most genealogists is to compile a detailed family history, or at least an extensive pedigree. Many never complete their research – not surprisingly, in view of the fact that one can never be certain that there are no more facts out there waiting to be found. Nevertheless, tens of thousands of pedigrees and family histories have been published and are to be found in libraries throughout the English-speaking world: the Society of Genealogists and the British Library have particularly substantial collections, as does the Library of Congress. Family history society journals are full of articles on particular families; many of the older genealogical journals, such as *Miscellanea genealogica et heraldica,* and *The Genealogist,* contain numerous pedigrees. Many books are devoted to pedigree collections. Most county historical and archaeological societies have printed numerous family histories in their transactions. Thousands of family histories have been published in book form, usually privately, although commercial publishers such as Phillimore do have a number of titles on their lists. In addition, numerous visitation returns compiled by the heralds of the College of Arms in the sixteenth and seventeenth centuries have been published by the Harleian Society; many of the latter have been reprinted on both fiche and CD (see the listings mentioned above). An attempt to list all of these is made in appropriate volumes of Raymonds *British genealogical library guides* series.

Most pedigrees published prior to 1975 are listed in one of the following titles:

- MARSHALL, G.W. *The genealogists guide.* 4th ed. Heraldry Today, 1967. Originally published 1903. For publications pre-1903.
- WHITMORE, J.B. *A genealogical guide: an index to British pedigrees in continuation of Marshalls genealogists guide.* Walford, 1953. Also published as Harleian Society **99, 101, 102 & 104.** For publications 1904-50.
- BARROW, G.B. *The genealogists guide: an index to printed British pedigrees and family histories, 1950-1975.* Research Publishing, 1977.

For pedigrees published post-1975, reliance must be placed on Raymond's county bibliographies, and on the digest section of *Family history news & digest.*

Biographical Dictionaries

How many family historians have undertaken a systematic check of biographical dictionaries in search of their ancestors? Such dictionaries abound, and contain a massive amount of information. If you are lucky enough to find an ancestor mentioned, then you will be rewarded with invaluable information for your family history. The *Dictionary of national biography* is to be found in most reference libraries, but it may not be realised that it represents just the tip of the iceberg. Biographical dictionaries contain millions of brief biographies of individuals who have been prominent in some way. Over 16,000 works are listed in:

- SLOCUM, R.B. *Biographical dictionaries and related works: an international bibliography ...* 2nd ed. Detroit: Gale Research, 1986.

Many of these dictionaries are indexed in:

- *Biography and genealogy master index: a consolidated index to more than 3,200,000 biographical sketches in over 350 current and retrospective biographical dictionaries.* 8 vols. Detroit: Gale, 1980. Supplements 1981-5, 1986-90, and annually from 1991. Also available on CD.

Some 324 of the most important British works have been microfilmed, and are available in major reference libraries as:
- *British biographical archive.* 1060 fiche. Munich: Saur, 1990.

Many other works in this field are listed in Raymond's *English genealogy* and his county bibliographies.

Local and County Histories

If you want to understand your family's pedigree in the context of the society in which your ancestors lived, you need to read histories of the places in which they resided. Innumerable county and local histories are available, although it remains the case that many parish histories remain to be written. Recent works of scholarship will provide you with a basic understanding of the background to your family's history; county and local histories of the 19th and early 20th centuries are more likely to provide you with the bare building blocks with which to construct pedigrees - transcripts of original sources such as wills, monumental inscriptions and parish register extracts, abound in them. Many 19th century histories may be identified in:

ANDERSON, JOHN P. *The book of British topography: a classified catalogue of the topographical works in the library of the British Museum ...* W.Satchell & Co., 1881. Reprinted Amsterdam: Theatrum Orbis Terrarum Ltd., 1966.

For works published since 1881, there is no single listing of local histories. Selected works are identified in Raymond's county bibliographies, but these are far from providing comprehensive listings. For some counties, comprehensive bibliographies of local histories are available; for others, you must check the catalogues of relevant local studies libraries. A full listing of county bibliographies cannot be given here; however, a few examples may be cited, illustrating the wide range of organizations responsible for producing such works:

CONISBEE, L.R. *A Bedfordshire bibliography, with some comments and biographical notes.* Bedfordshire Historical Record Society, 1962.

Abbots Bickington to Zeal Monachorum: a handlist of Devon parish histories. Exeter: Devon County Council Libraries, 1994.

POWELL, W.R. *A history of the County of Essex: bibliography.* Oxford University Press, 1959. Supplement, 1987.

DOUCH, ROBERT. *A handbook of local history, Dorset, with a supplement of additions and corrections to 1960.* Bristol: University of Bristol Dept. of Extra-Mural Studies, 1962.

9. Conclusion

This is far from being a comprehensive treatise on the subject of genealogical books and libraries; there are many other points that could have been made, and many other topics, for example, school registers, migration, palaeography, have not even been mentioned. The aim has been to provide you with an introduction to the idea that the pursuit of genealogy should be as much book-based as it is archive-based. Genealogists can find a great deal to interest them in books and libraries, and it is hoped that you have been provided with some clues to enable you to pursue your genealogical inquiries.

Every good genealogical book ends with a bibliography identifying further reading. In the case of the present work, the further reading consists of the entire literature of English genealogy, much of which can be identified by referring to the books listed on the back cover. Many of the themes treated here are considered at greater length in:

- WINTERBOTHAM, DIANA, & CROSBY, ALAN. *The local studies library: a handbook for local historians.* British Association for Local History, 1998.

Stuart Raymond